Alaskan Night Before CHRISTMAS

Alaskan Night Before CHRISTMAS

By Tricia Brown

Illustrated by Alan Stacy

PELICAN PUBLISHING COMPANY

GRETNA 2013

*In memory of Alaska pioneers Con and Nellie Miller, who built
Santa Claus House and founded North Pole, Alaska.
—T. B.*

*For Dad and all the wonderful adventures we had together in Alaska
—A.F.S.*

First printing, July 2008
Second printing, September 2009
Third printing, September 2013

*The word "Pelican" and the depiction of a pelican are trademarks
of Pelican Publishing Company, Inc., and are registered in the
U.S. Patent and Trademark Office.*

Library of Congress Cataloging-in-Publication Data

Brown, Tricia.
 Alaskan night before Christmas / by Tricia Brown ; illustrated by Alan Stacy.
  p. cm.
 ISBN-13: 978-1-58980-554-5 (alk. paper) 1. Christmas—Juvenile poetry. 2. Alaska—
Juvenile poetry. 3. Santa Claus—Juvenile poetry. 4. Caribou—Juvenile poetry. 5. Children's
poetry, American. I. Stacy, Alan, ill. II. Title.
 PS3602.R7235A79 2008
 811'.6—dc22

                    2008002457

Printed in Malaysia
Published by Pelican Publishing Company, Inc.
1000 Burmaster Street, Gretna, Louisiana 70053

'Twas the night before Christmas
In the famed Last Frontier,
Where the northern lights shimmer,
Through skies crisp and clear.

At North Pole, Alaska, the work was all done
Under brilliant white spotlights, no sign of
   the sun.
Now doubling the pace, elves toiled into night
To load up the sled for a long winter's flight.

Talk about cold!
  Near forty below!
But jolly old Santa could
  go with the flow.
    He'd plugged in the sled, changed
      out the used oil,
Had the ice scraper packed, grill
    covered with foil.

The rig now was full; the Big Man stood ready.
He called to his flyers, urging all to hold steady.
(Yet it's not like you've heard. The crew didn't consist
Of eight miniature reindeer—here's the story you missed.)

At the head of the team stood a proud-
  looking critter
With dinner-plate hooves and white fur on
  his sitter.
In the prime of his life, antlers ample in size,
A fine rack to spar other bucks for a prize.

Kotzebue the Caribou, named for the town
Near the sweep of the Circle 'cross Kotzebue Sound.
Glad of his calling—no pet deer was he.
Kotz and his kin were wanderers, the free.

His hackles had risen when he first heard the story
Of eight tiny reindeer . . . "Oh, blast it to glory!"
"I'm a *'boo,* not a reindeer," he said with insistence.
But in spite of his words, he'd met much resistance.

Every Christmas the stories were told and retold
Of Santa and reindeer—the lies that were sold!
Kids never grew tired of that sorry tall tale.
Cartoons about Rudolph reran without fail.

Now this certain year, vain Kotzebue yearned
To fix unclear thinking where deer were concerned.
Kotz wanted that glory; he wanted the fame.
He wanted a carol that featured his name.

Sure, Kotz was stuck up, but he wasn't all bad.
He just wanted attention if there was some to
  be had.
And Christmas was perfect for grabbing the light.
Which he did all year long when a tourist he'd sight.

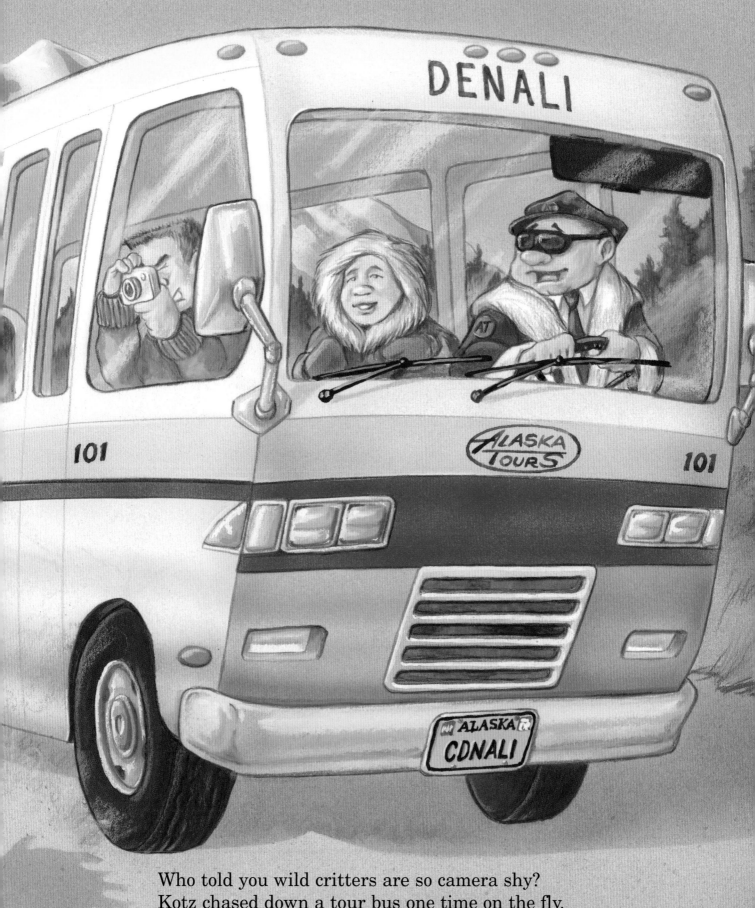

Who told you wild critters are so camera shy?
Kotz chased down a tour bus one time on the fly.
He'd galloped behind them, *"Look at me, look at me."*
The driver then spied him and slowed down to see.

And not long ago, Santa'd asked the whole group
To line up according to alphabet soup.
Kotz told the others they'd learned it all wrong.
"It's the KBCs, not ABCs. You know that great song!?"

Now back to our story of one solemn night
When all were preparing to head out in flight.
Kotz positioned himself in the number-one post.
If a camera crew showed, he'd give them the most.

This particular year, he'd groomed extra long.
He'd been working out daily to look extra strong.
He wondered if radar would show his best side,
Convinced that this Christmas, he'd be hitting
  his stride.

Before they left town, Santa bumped through
  his list
Of caribou names that made his tongue twist.
He'd named them himself for towns of the North,
But he fumbled each Christmas 'ere time to
  go forth.

"Now Kotzebue, now Kvichak, now Egegik and Ekwok,
On Tuluksak, on Togiak, on Nuiqsut and Newtok.
From the top of the world to the heart of each kid,
Let's fill up their eyes with the treasures they bid!"

Away they all went, with Kotz in the lead.
He'd sent out releases for media feed.
At New York and London, Paris and Rome,
He'd planned a press conference before heading home.

In his head danced ideas, so unChristmaslike,
Of me-first and stardom, of bright city lights.
So distracted was he by his self-centered thoughts
That the team became lost thanks to big-headed Kotz.

Down through the ice fog, they went for a look.
A mountain? A signpost? Perhaps a guidebook?
Spiraling, hunting, a landmark they sought
To reset their bearings, but all seemed for naught.

Santa's eyes, how they squinted, his hands, how
    they gripped.
In the lead, Kotz just sprinted, while his pride
    slightly dipped.
Just then the fog parted, and the team spied a place
For landing unnoticed, as they tried to save face.

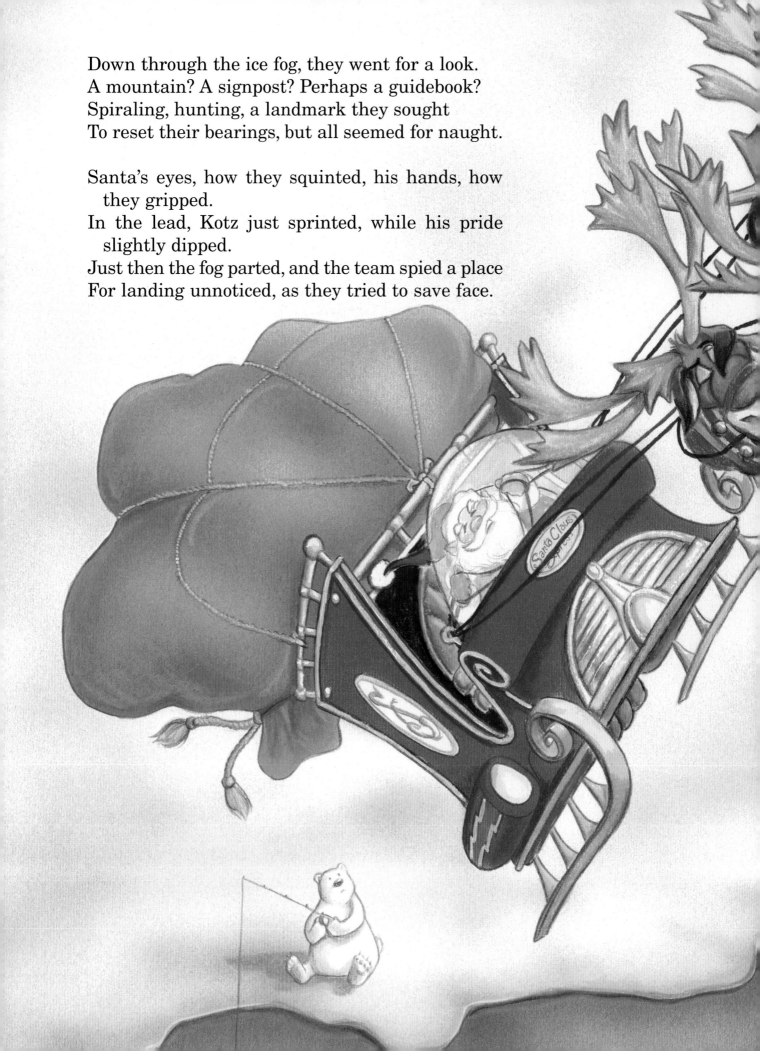

Much to Santa's surprise, they hadn't gone far.
   They set down in Anchorage, where a reindeer
      named Star
      Had spent his young life in a pen at the zoo,
Never hearing of Santa or vain Kotzebue.

In true northern spirit, Star gave his best treats,
A map, a clean bathroom, a zoo mug, some eats.
Humble and sharing, so unlike our Kotz,
Star hosted a feast: "Please eat more. I have lots."

The 'boo wasn't humbled by all this good grace.
Kotz snubbed the nice reindeer—and right to his face.
"See ya later, short stuff. Time to go meet the press.
Plus we've gotta 'do' Christmas, for the kids, more or less."

Santa heard the exchange and was shocked to the core
He'd had it with Kotz—this 'boo was a bore.
He called a "Time Out" to nip bad behavior
On this eve that's to welcome the birth of the Savior.

Saying, "See you tomorrow," he swapped Kotz
  for Star
Who was such a sweet servant, loving, unmarred
By puffed-up importance in this holy season.
Every Christmas from then, Kotz remembered
  the reason.

In the end, the great Kotz spent a night at the zoo,
And the zookeeper wondered if Star had the flu.
And the press wrote again about reindeer in lead.
And Kotzebue the Caribou learned a lesson indeed.

Kotz lost his swell gig, 'twas a wonderful living,
Just 'cause he was big . . . on taking, not giving.

Santa named his caribou after real towns and villages in Alaska. Here's how to pronounce their names correctly (even though Santa still can't manage):

Kotzebue	KOTS-a-bew
Kvichak	QUEE-jack
Egegik	IG-gah-gik
Ekwok	ECK-wok
Tuluksak	TOO-luke-sack
Togiak	TOE-gee-yack
Nuiqsut	NOOK-soot
Newtok	NEW-tock

Did you know? The word *'boo* is short for caribou among many Alaskans. In the Inupiaq Eskimo language, *tutu* is the word for caribou. It means "the wanderer." Caribou and reindeer are cousins—although they look different, genetically they are part of the same family. Males and females grow antlers. Wild caribou are bigger and ever on the move as they migrate in huge herds. Domesticated reindeer are slightly smaller and raised by Alaska Native herders, mostly on the Seward Peninsula.